PHONICS CONNECTIONS

At a Fire

by Rachel Mann

capstone classroom

Oh, no! A home is on fire. Who will help stop the flames?

Brave firefighters will help. They can save the home from the fire.

The firefighters race to the pole. They grab their hats and coats.

The men and women hop on a red fire engine. They drive fast to the blaze.

The firefighters can smell the smoke!
A firefighter goes up the ladder.

Another firefighter uses a fire hose.
He wets the hot flames with water.

The fire is out. The heroes save the home!